A New Time and A New Place

To all Anna's and my children...
...a growing number we could not have imagined
when we began our life together in July of 1954.

4 children
11 grandchildren
and to date,
12 great-grandchildren

A New Time and A New Place
© 2012 by Jack Hayford

Cover Illustration by Sylvia Corbett
Book Design by Michelle Glush

ISBN: 978091684740-1

Printed in the United States of America

Most Scripture quotations are from:
The New King James Version (NKJV) ©1984 by Thomas Nelson, Inc.

Also quoted:
The Holy Bible, New International Version (NIV)
© 1973, 1984 by International Bible Society, used by permission of
Zondervan Publishing House

Scripture quotations marked (NLT) are taken from The Holy Bible, New
Living Translation, © 1996. Used by permission of Tyndale House Pub-
lishers, Inc. Wheaten, Illinois 60189. All rights reserved.

For more information:
Jack Hayford Ministries • 14800 Sherman Way, Van Nuys, CA 91405
www.jackhayford.org

Contents

A Wrong Turn... and a Right One

Now it came to pass, in the days when the judges ruled that there was a famine in the land. And a certain man of Bethlehem, Judah went to sojourn in the country of Moab, he and his wife and two sons. The name of the man was Elimelech, and the name of his wife was Naomi, and the names of his two sons were Mahlon and Chilion—Ephrathites of Bethlehem, Judah. And they went to the country of Moab and remained there. Then Elimelech, Naomi's husband, died; and she was left, and her two sons. Now they took wives of the women of Moab: the name of one was Orpah, and the name of the other Ruth. And they dwelt there about ten years. Then both Mahlon and Chilion also died; so the woman survived her two sons and her husband.

Then she rose with her daughters-in-law that she might return from the country of Moab, for she had heard in the country of Moab that the Lord had visited His people by giving them bread. Therefore, she went out from the place where she was, and her two daughters-in-law with her; and they went on the way to return to the land of Judah. And Naomi said to her two daughters-in-law, "Go, return each to her mother's house. The Lord deal kindly with you, as you have dealt with the dead and with me. The Lord grant that you may find rest, each in the house of her husband." So she kissed them, and they lifted up their voices and wept. And they said to her, "Surely, we will return with you to your people." But Naomi said, "Turn back my daughters; why will you go with me? Are there still sons in my womb, that they may be your husbands? Turn back, my daughters, go—for I am too old to have a husband. If I should say I have hope, if I should have a husband tonight and should also bear sons, would you wait for them till they were grown? Would you restrain yourselves from having husbands? No, my daughters; for it grieves me very much for your sakes that the hand of the Lord has gone out against me." Then they lifted up their voices and wept again; and Orpah kissed her mother-in-law, but Ruth clung to her.

And she said, "Look, your sister-in-law has gone back to her people and to her gods; return after your sister-in-law." But Ruth said,

"Entreat me not to leave you,
Or to turn back from following after you;
For wherever you go, I will go;
And wherever you lodge, I will lodge.
Your people shall be my people,

And your God, my God.
Where you die I will die,
And there will I be buried.
The Lord do so to me, and more also,
If anything but death parts you and me.

When she saw that she was determined to go with her, she stopped speaking to her.

Now the two of them went until they came to Bethlehem. And it happened, when they had come to Bethlehem, that all the city was excited because of them; and the women said, "Is this Naomi?" But she said to them, "Do not call me Naomi; call me Mara, for the Almighty has dealt very bitterly with me. I went out full, and the Lord has brought me home again empty. Why do you call me Naomi, since the Lord has testified against me, and the Almighty has afflicted me?"

So Naomi returned, and Ruth the Moabitess her daughter-in-law with her, who returned from the country of Moab. Now they came to Bethlehem at the beginning of barley harvest. (Ruth 1)

$\mathcal{A}$ WRONG TURN…AND A RIGHT ONE

It all began with a wrong turn.

But for the grace of God, the story could have ended as it began…in tragedy, bitterness, and death.

But God had something else in mind. And because He did, we have one of the most beautiful love stories ever told. But more than an account of a man, a woman, and a romance, it is the story of a God who seeks what was lost and redeems what was forsaken.

✦ ✦ ✦

The Book of Ruth is a true story, a thin slice of real history. But like so much of biblical history, it speaks to us of God's ways with people…people like you and me. The apostle Paul assures us that we can find wisdom, comfort, and hope by giving careful thought to God's ways with His people in times gone by. He writes:

For whatever things were written before were written for our learning, that we through the patience and comfort of the Scriptures might have hope. (Romans 15:4)

There is all of that in the Book of Ruth. Learning. Patience. Comfort. And certainly hope. Ruth was a woman who came to a new time and to a new place, and in her experience, there is a message for all of us. The Lord is calling each one of us to a new time and a new place. And how we respond to His call will not only determine the character of our days here on earth, it will determine our very destiny.

The Book of Ruth tells the story of how a Gentile, a girl from Moab, came to be the great-grandmother of Israel's most celebrated king...and entered the bloodline of the King of kings.

The opening words give us the setting.. *"Now it came to pass, in the days when the judges ruled."* Historically, this was between 1,200 and 1,300 B.C.—one of the most tumultuous times in Israel's long, troubled history. The wasting famine described in the first verse of the story may have been the least of Israel's problems. It was an era marked by violence, oppression, bloodshed, and unbelievable lawlessness.

The last verse of the Book of Judges is very explicit about this:

In those days there was no king in Israel; everyone did what was right in his own eyes. (Judges 21:25)

The law of God meant little or nothing—even to those known as the people of God. The people who claimed relationship with God had become a law unto themselves.

Right in the midst of this dark, chaotic epoch, we're given the story of a man, his wife, and his two boys… one young father looking for a new time and a new place. But on his own terms.

✦ ✦ ✦

Elimelech was a citizen of Bethlehem, but at that point in history, the fact meant little. It was just an obscure village. As Micah would later describe it, one of "the thousands in Judah" (Micah 5:2). Its only significance was that it lay within the boundaries of God's appointed inheritance for His people.

The story begins with a fateful decision. A wrong turn. In the grinding anxiety and suffering of a national drought, and in a quest to elevate his family's circumstance, Elimelech made a momentous choice: He moved from Israel to Moab, a neighboring nation. It was neither a good decision or a wise move.

Yet what he did is one of those things we are all sometimes inclined to do under the stress of circumstances; we are tempted to step outside the circle of God's promise and seek solutions to our problems on our own terms. And like Elimelech and his family, we find emptiness and heartache rather than the relief and fulfillment we longed for.

The Bible says, "There is a way that seems right to a man, but its end is the way of death" (Proverbs 14:12). The significance of Elimelech's decision to leave—not only Bethlehem and Judah but the borders of Israel itself—is that a man under duress went looking for an answer *outside* the boundaries of God's provision for His people. It was a way that seemed right to him, but it ended in his death.

Elimelech left Bethlehem, "the house of Bread." He left Israel, the land of promise, to seek a new life outside the inheritance of his people. As someone in our era might phrase it, he went looking for a life in all the wrong places. Elimelech's name means "the Lord is my King." Yet his life story became a contradiction of that name.

Somehow, I don't believe Elimelech's decision to pull up stakes and leave Israel was an impulsive, fly-by-night whim. Yes, there must have been a morning when he woke up, rolled over in bed, and for the first time said to Naomi, "I've been thinking about moving the family to Moab." But long before that moment, the man had considered his circumstances and weighed his options.

He pondered it, and the more he thought about it, the more moving to Moab seemed the plausible and practical thing to do. In that very fact, we face a demanding dilemma that has confronted believers since time out of memory. *What do I do when the ways and promises of the Lord do not answer to human logic or rationale?*

Please notice, I didn't say God's ways are illogical or irrational. They're not. But they are *different*. And so very, very often they don't square with our common sense or track with our lines of reason. That ought not to surprise us, however, since our Lord Himself asserts that. Through Isaiah, He affirms,

"For My thoughts are not your thoughts,
Nor are your ways My ways...
For as the heavens are higher than the earth,
So are My ways higher than your ways,
And My thoughts than your thoughts."
(Isaiah 55:8-9)

The New Testament declares the same thing in our era. The apostle Paul describes the Lord's judgments are "unsearchable" and His ways "past finding out" (Romans 11:33). He is simply underlining what the Savior Himself said. In presenting His own teaching, Jesus time and again challenged human systems of reason: "You have heard that it was said…*but I say unto you…*"

Sooner or later we need to come to terms with this dilemma; God's ways…or mine? And wisdom recommends we learn to align ourselves with God's thoughts and ways. It is crucial not only to our growth as believers, but to our fulfillment as the Father's children. I need to teach myself to say, "Yes, this seems like a good and sensible course of action on the surface…but what does the Father have to say? What is His mind on this thing?" As Paul wrote to the Ephesians, "Find out what pleases the Lord" (Ephesians 5:10 NIV). His word of promise, His law of wisdom, and His Spirit's prompting within—when allowed reign *over* and *above* my mind—have a way of nudging me beyond the limits of human "sense" toward the horizons of holy "hope."

James addressed a group of people who were probably going through trials as serious and heartbreaking as Elimelech's. Yet even in the midst of that pressure and stress, the apostle assured them that God's wisdom was readily available. "If any of you lacks wisdom," he wrote, "let him ask of God, who gives to all liberally and without reproach, and it will be given to him" (James 1:5).

We have no indication that Elimelech ever sought the Lord's mind in the matter of this move—or even sought the Lord at all. His life speaks to us of spiritual people who function only at a rational level. He speaks to us of believers who rely solely on human logic rather than the direction and counsel of God's Word and God's Spirit.

Am I arguing for irrational practices or behavior? No. But for those who would know the Lord's purpose and blessing in their lives, "reason" and "rationality" must be predicated on inviolable spiritual principles. There are spiritual boundaries for the inheritance of God's people that must not be transgressed. And when we are considering any major change or decision in our lives, we must make certain that our "sensible," "practical" plans have first been laid at His feet. If He is really Lord—the supreme authority of our lives, He must be given veto power over *all* of our own designs and schemes. Once granted, the dilemma of decision making is resolved.

In Elimelech's case, there was a powerful argument for human reasoning. After all, *it only made sense* to escape the famine. *It only made sense* to move to Moab.

Yet Scripture tells us clearly that when famines— *dry times*—come into our lives, the Lord will make it His business to care for those who *rest* their hope in Him rather than *rush* to figure out their own solutions.

David enunciated this in a number of ways in the psalms:

Behold, the eye of the Lord is on those who fear Him.
On those who hope in His mercy,
To deliver their soul from death,
And to keep them alive in famine.
                    (Psalm 33:18-19)

The Lord knows the days of the upright,
And their inheritance shall be forever.
They shall not be ashamed in the evil time,
And in the days of famine they shall be satisfied. ...

I have been young, and now am old;
Yet I have not seen the righteous forsaken,
Nor his descendants begging bread.
                    (Psalm 37:18-19, 25)

The message is clear and simple. God would have taken care of Elimelech and his family if they had stayed in Israel. The Lord promises He will faithfully deal with the people who stand firmly with Him—even when they are lacking what their hearts desire.

In our own experience of life, you and I may never face agricultural famine, but our "hungers" encompass more than food. All of us hunger in different ways. We hunger for acceptance. We hunger for vocational fulfillment. We hunger for recognition. We hunger for sufficiency and adequacy, whether it's in the performance of duty or in the availability of resources. And society *incessantly* strums the strings of one of our most vulnerable human desires—our sexual hungers.

Within all this, how often do you find yourself hungering for "something different" in your life? A change of scene. A change of circumstances. A change of pace. It's a typical attitude here in southern California, where I make my home. You hear it often: "I'm tired of the smog, the traffic, and the freeways! I'm sick of my job and disgusted with the rat race. I'm moving to Oregon!" (Or Montana or Manitoba or wherever.)

Now moving yourself or your family may not be quite the same as moving to Moab. And I'm neither arguing against moving to another state nor saying that California is the promised land. But I am suggesting that geographic moves aren't the answer people may think them to be. Loading up a U-Haul and moving to another city or another state will never remedy an empty heart or a restless spirit.

At other times, people think they can scratch their inner itches by changing their image...changing their wardrobes...changing their cars...changing their careers...or even changing their wives or husbands. *But the Spirit's words in the Word of God warn us against looking for inner peace and satisfaction by making external changes!*

Only the Lord can bring about true change or genuine fulfillment, and He does it from the inside out. He alone can satisfy a restless heart, but He cannot bless us when we violate His word or His principles to chase idle dreams stimulated by inner cravings. The end result of those pursuits will be an even deeper sense of emptiness and frustration instead of the satisfaction we desire. Nevertheless...there is an Elimelech alive in all of us, looking for a new time and a new place, on his own terms. His reasoning usually sounds something like this:

- (To a married person.) "Your spouse isn't fulfilling your emotional or sexual needs...so you deserve— no, *need!*—those secret fantasies of yours. You *need* that pornography or that adulterous affair."

- (To a single person.) "It's evident God isn't going to provide you with a Christian mate. (How long have you waited?) So get real! Take whatever looks good to you—pagan, plain 'nice' person, or whomever. It'll work out in time!"

You'll hear the whisper of the Elimelech spirit in your own rationalizations...

- when you cut ethical corners or cheat in business or rack up an impossible debt while arguing that expenditure is the key to "changing" your future.

- when you know the video you've rented wouldn't be pleasing to the Lord Jesus yet you tell yourself, "Hey, this is my world. And besides, I'm bored and need a little excitement."
- when you dabble in drink or drugs, saying, "I know this shouldn't be part of my life as a believer, but I can't face my circumstances without them right now."

We sell ourselves on our need to "help God work things out." We argue our need to make a change, add some excitement, or get something new going, because we're empty. Our tastes just aren't being satisfied where we are and with what we have. But the problem is deeper than an earthly "taste" can satisfy. Jesus calls you and me "people of the light"—"children of the day." He longs to wean us from dabbling in the darkness and points the way to a re-sensitizing of our taste buds. His supply for that hollowness within is a joy that only He can provide.

Our Lord told His followers, "My joy in you will make your joy complete." He prayed to the Father for a *full measure* of joy within them (see John 15:11; 17:13). Paul saw the point so clearly that he repeated the call to joy three times for the Philippians...

Finally, my brethren, rejoice in the Lord!... Rejoice in the

Lord always. Again I will say, rejoice!
(Philippians 3:1; 4:4)

Though he was confident of God's grace working in the lives of believers, he realized the pressures they face living in the midst of a "crooked and perverse generation, among which you shine as lights in the world" (Philippians 2:15). He knew that to shine like lights in a dark place—to actually *glow* in contrast to the dreary sameness of a Christless world—a resource greater than religiousness was needed.

Paul recognized what we may sometimes forget: Being surrounded by darkness can create an appetite for shadows. And even those who belong to the light may succumb to their light being dimmed or smothered and their tastes jaded by a society that lives in the dark.

So what was Paul's solution? *Rejoice!* And then rejoice some more! Why? Because he knew that there is an energy in praise that brings the glow of God's glory to our lives and burns out all remaining traces of darkness. "The joy of the Lord is your strength!" (Nehemiah 8:10).

Elimelech is a case study of a man who allowed his life to become dominated by doubt in an atmosphere of discouragement. Similarly, Christians begin to hunger for foods of a "far country" rather than being satisfied with Christ when we fail to recognize the *causes* of our hunger and our emptiness. It isn't our problems that make us feel empty; it is the failure to enjoy God's presence. It is the simple neglect of a daily, hour-by-hour, moment-by-moment walk with Jesus Himself. And when we neglect His Word and our conversation with Him, we inevitably begin to tolerate unconfessed sin in our lives, grieving and quenching His Spirit within us.

As a result, we feel the emptiness, we feel the sadness, we sense the void. *Of course* we do! But, instead of hurrying back to Him to cleanse our hearts and meet our needs, we stray over the boundaries. We slip over the border. We wander outside of our inheritance. We cultivate a taste for the bread of Moab, rather than "the bread which came down from heaven" (John 6:41).

Outside the boundaries of the covenant, you and I will ultimately find what Elimelech, Mahlon, and Chilion found—death. The untimely passing of these men is not an act of an angry God but the result of the *withering of life* in but one of the many ways things *"die"* without the sustaining life of our Creator

Jesus, who *calls* us into life, calls us within *specific boundaries*. He has a new time and a new place for each one of us, but only on *His* terms, not ours. The Bible says some very pointed things about how believers are to live and to move. Elimelech is a man who chased a rainbow and lost an inheritance. He took his family with him, and they lost everything too—including him. Before the lost could be redeemed, someone needed to retrace that costly journey and return to the place of blessing.

And someone did.

But she didn't go alone.

◆ ◆ ◆

Naomi said, "I'm going home."

She had no reason to stay in Moab. She had heard, as verse 6 puts it, "that the Lord had visited His people by giving them bread." It moves me to consider that Elimelech missed out on that visitation. When it came, he wasn't there to receive it. Turning his back on his inheritance, he went seeking what the Lord (in His time) had intended to provide all along. By trying to provide for himself, Elimelech missed the provision of God.

So Naomi loaded up her meager belongings and turned her face once again toward Israel. There is no real reason for Orpah and Ruth, her daughters-in-law, to go with her. Their husbands, Naomi's sons, were dead. In Israel, they would be strangers and foreigners.

As the young women began to follow her, Naomi turned to them and graciously released them. "You go on back," she told them. "You've been kind to me through these years, and now I pray that my God will be kind to you. Go back to your family homes, and—who knows? You may soon find new husbands." Scripture says she kissed them and they wept.

By releasing them, Naomi gave them freedom to stay in their homeland. Orpah tearfully accepted that release and walked out of the pages of Scripture, never to be mentioned again.

The whole story of the book hinges on the fact that Ruth *did not.*

Not knowing what hardships or heartaches lay ahead of her in a foreign land, she chose to cling to what was left of her new family rather than returning to the old. In so doing, she placed herself in a position to find a new time and a new place.

When Ruth spoke these words that have become classic and so familiar, she was simply living out a sense of commitment.

"Entreat me not to leave you,
Or to turn back from following after you;
For wherever you go, I will go;
And wherever you lodge, I will lodge.
Your people shall be my people,
And your God, my God.
Where you die I will die,

And there will I be buried.
The Lord do so to me, and more also,
If anything but death parts you and me.

✦ ✦ ✦

Make no mistake, this was an enormous decision for this young woman. As far as she knew, nothing was waiting for her in Israel. No land. No inheritance. No provision. No future husband. No future children. In all of that nation, she would know only one person: her elderly mother-in-law. There wouldn't even be an Orpah to share the strangeness of a new land.

Yet there was one thing.

She had heard her husband and his family talk about a God in Israel.

A God who had a famous name

A powerful God.

A holy God.

A God who had shielded and delivered His people again and again.

Though she may have had only a few distorted pictures of that God, she had made up her mind to pursue Him. She told Naomi, "I want that God to be my God. I want to be in the land where you're going and where

He dwells. Where you're going, that's where I'm going."

The Bible says she *clung* to Naomi. She wasn't about to be turned away.

♦ ♦ ♦

If you and I would truly move ahead with the Lord into a new time and a new place, we must expect Him to point out those things in our lives that obstruct our entry. And that, dear one, may be painful.

Each one of us has experienced the touch of God on unyielded areas of our lives...areas where He wants to work a new depth of character, a new point of commitment, a new adjustment of our thoughts. The Lord is neither unkind nor a hard taskmaster. But He knows there is no way for me to get from point A to point B in His purpose, apart from something happening *in* me. That "something" is described by one word in the Bible and one word only.

It's the word *repent*.

Although the word conjures up images of soapbox oratory, street-corner prophets, and the sawdust trail, to repent simply means to change your mind. To change your direction. You are headed down one road, and you stop in your tracks, turn around, and head down another. That's how we each begin with Christ, but it's also an ongoing process. In each of our lives there are things the Lord wants to deal with. Hidden bastions of pride. Lingering habits of the flesh. Gaps in our discipline. Hardening in our attitudes. Cooling in our zeal.

These junctures in our lives are very much like the crossroads that Ruth and Orpah faced. The Lord comes to us to lead us to a new level of service, a new level of fellowship with Him, a new level of maturity. How will we respond? Well, we might answer as Ruth did, saying, "Lord, I don't know what's ahead, but I'm ready to go, clinging only to You." But then again, we may be tempted to give Orpah's response: "Well, I feel bad about having to make this decision, but I'm going to stick it out in good old Moab."

Oh, Orpah was certainly *sorry*. She felt a pang of regret. The parting made her wistful and blue. But this type of sorrow produces very little change or fruitfulness. It's not the "godly sorrow" that Paul saw in the Corinthians—the type of sorrow that really brings a change of heart (2 Corinthians 7:10-11). It's more like a vague depression that goes nowhere at all.

There is in every one of us an Orpah who will sigh, dab her eyes, and say, "Oh, I feel so bad. I feel so sorry. Following God to a new time and a new place sounds nice. But I think I'll just stay where I am. After all, it's what I know. It's where I'm comfortable."

In such a way, Orpah slipped out the back door to Moab, her eyes on the old landmarks, her feet treading easily in the well-worn path.

Let's take a different course! Let's walk in the footsteps of a courageous young foreigner named Ruth. No, her way wasn't easy at all. The path she began to walk must have torn her heart with uncertainties about the future. Nevertheless, she chose the costly course of commitment.

And it lead to a new time and a new place.

◆ ◆ ◆

So it was that two made their way into that little town of Bethlehem rather than one. For Naomi, it was a homecoming. But not a joyful one. As the widow and her foreign daughter-in-law walked down the main street, the women gathered around the travelers. This was a bit of excitement in a hamlet where excitement may have been rare.

"Could this be Naomi?" they asked.

Naomi shook her head sadly.

"Do not call me Naomi; call me Mara, for the Almighty has dealt very bitterly with me. I went out full, and the Lord has brought me home again empty. Why do you call me Naomi, since the Lord has testified against me,

and the Almighty has afflicted me?" (vv. 20-21)

Naomi had lots of miles and plenty of time to practice her little homecoming speech. "Don't call me Naomi, or 'Pleasant,'" she said. "That was someone else from years ago. Call me what I am. *Mara.* A bitter woman. What else could I be? The Almighty Himself has dealt bitterly with me."

As you read her remarks, another curious trait appears—and one to which we are all vulnerable. You can't help but notice one little word that keeps repeating itself.

Me, me, me, me.

Naomi certainly believed in the Lord. She just didn't believe He cared much for *her.* She was so focused on herself and her loss she couldn't see anything of the Lord's grace and kindness toward her. The truth was, the Lord was about to open the floodgates of blessing on her life.

And indeed, He had already blessed her.

Think about it. Had she really come home "empty"? What about that attractive, clear-eyed, young woman who walked by her side and who had given up everything to follow her and be with her? What of Ruth's loving sacrifice to be Naomi's companion? As the woman would later say, Ruth was "better to her than seven sons" (4:15). But right then, Naomi couldn't see any of that.

To her, everything looked black. That's what self-pity can do to any of us. We become so obsessed with what we've missed or what we've lost that we no longer have eyes to see the wonderful provision we *have*, or the hope dawning just outside our shuttered windows.

Still, there is one thing we can say for Naomi. Even in her gloom and bitterness and loss, *she went back to the right place*. She was "blessable," because she returned to the place of blessing.

Ruth, in the meantime, must have been looking about her with wide eyes. Everything seemed so strange and new. Yet she would soon begin to discover what I think every one of us wants to find: the freshness and newness of God's best for our lives—and the excitement of living out God's gracious purpose.

Hear me, dear one. Our Lord offers you and me the same fresh newness, too. But we'll never find it on our own terms. That was Elimelech's way, and it dead-ended in an alien land. Ruth, however, set out in faith for a place she had never been and chose God's terms, not her own.

That's the path of success for you and me, too. At the heart of it all, you'll find these words: "Lord, where You go, I'll go. Where You live, I'll live. I'll be one of Your people, and You shall be my Father God. And Jesus, where You died at the cross, I'll die there, too, and I'm going to live with You and because of You."

Ruth bound her commitment with an oath. When she said, "The Lord do so to me and more also if I don't do that," she was really saying, "May God judge me if I don't abide by this commitment."

The Lord knows how to hold us to our commitments. He will bring stern but loving correction into the lives of His children who continue to walk outside of His boundaries (see Hebrews 12:4-13). He'll correct us so we're aware that we're violating the boundaries and so we may return to walk again in obedience and blessing.

"I have been young," wrote the psalmist, "and now an old; yet I have not seen the righteous forsaken, nor his descendants begging bread" (Psalm 37:25).

Those words were spoken by the great-grandson of a woman who left a country outside of covenant boundaries to come within them, and found new life. And what she found there stood in stark contrast to the era of the judges, where people made up their own rules, did whatever they wanted to do, and paid little heed to God.

Ruth had a different spirit. She said, "I will embrace the living Lord and find His Way." In finding it, she stepped into a future legacy beyond imagination. One day in the future, Ruth's multiple-times-great-grandson would be born as a baby in that same Bethlehem town where she began her sojourn as a stranger.

And this descendent of a Moabite girl would be

called Jesus the Christ, the Son of the living God! Who could have dreamed it? But it truly happened, and the story of Ruth has become a profile of faith and courage for us all.

Once upon a time, a foreigner walked out of the shadows, out of the presence of death, and came into a new time and place.

Let her story be yours as well.

A NEW TIME AND A NEW PLACE

Chapter Two

A New Relationship

There was a relative of Naomi's husband, a man of great wealth, of the family of Elimelech. His name was Boaz. So Ruth the Moabitess said to Naomi, "Please let me go to the field and glean the heads of grain after him in whose sight I may find favor." And she said to her, "Go, my daughter." Then she left, and went and gleaned in the field after the reapers. And she happened to come to the part of the field belonging to Boaz, who was of the family of Elimelech.

Now behold, Boaz came from Bethlehem, and said to the reapers, "The Lord be with you!" And they answered him, "The Lord bless you!" Then Boaz said to his servant who was in charge of the reapers, "Whose young woman is this?" So the servant who was in charge of the reapers answered and said, "It is the young Moabite woman who came back with Naomi from the country of Moab. And she said, 'Please let me glean and gather after the reapers among the sheaves.' So she came and has continued from morning until now, though she rested a little in the house."

Then Boaz said to Ruth, "You will listen, my daughter, will you not? Do not go to glean in another field, nor go from here, but stay close by my young women. Let your eyes be on the field which they reap, and go after them. Have I not commanded the young men not to touch you? And when you are thirsty, go to the vessels and drink from what the men have drawn." So she fell on her face, bowed to the ground, and said to him, "Why have I found favor in your eyes, that you should take notice of me, since I am a foreigner?" And Boaz answered and said to her, "It has been fully reported to me, all that you have done for your mother-in-law since the death of your husband, and how you have left your father and your mother in the land of you birth, and have come to a people whom you did not know before. The Lord repay your work, and a full reward be given you by the Lord God of Israel, under whose wings you have come for refuge." Then she said, "Let me find favor in your sight, my lord; for you have comforted me, and have spoken kindly to your maidservant, though I am not like one of your maidservants.

Now Boaz said to her at mealtime, "Come here, and eat of the bread, and dip your piece of bread in the vinegar." So she sat beside the reapers, and he passed the parched grain to her; and she ate and was satisfied, and kept some back. And when she rose up to glean, Boaz commanded his young men, saying, "Let her glean even among the sheaves, and do not reproach her. And let some grain from the bundles fall *purposely for her; leave it that she may glean, and do not rebuke her."*

So she gleaned in the field until evening, and beat out what she had gleaned, and it was about an ephah of barley. [That would be enough to feed her and Naomi about five days, so it was an amazing amount for a gleaner to gather.] *Then she took it up and went into the city, and her mother-in-law saw what she had gleaned. So she brought out and gave to her what she had kept back after she had been satisfied. And her mother-in-law said to her, "Where have you gleaned today? And where did you work? Blessed be the one who took notice of you." So she told her mother-in-law with whom she had worked, and said, "The man's name with whom I worked today is Boaz." Then Naomi said to her daughter-in-law, "Blessed be he of the Lord, who has not forsaken His kindness to the living and the dead!" And Naomi said to her, "This man is a relative of ours, one of our near kinsmen." Ruth the Moabitess said, "He also said to me, 'You shall stay close by my young men until they have finished all my harvest.'" And Naomi said to Ruth her daughter-in-law, "It is good, my daughter, that you go out with his young women, and that people do not meet you in any other field." So she stayed close by the young women of Boaz, to glean until the end of the barley harvest and wheat harvest; and she dwelt with her mother-in-law.* (Ruth 2)

A NEW RELATIONSHIP

Ruth's determination to follow Naomi was the pivot upon which her life turned. On the strength of that commitment she was brought to a new time and a new place...and found a new love.

Ruth, of course, had no idea what would open up as a result of her decision. In her wildest imagination, she couldn't have dreamed what would flow out of her choice at the desert crossroads. All she knew was—come what may—she'd made up her mind about her life's direction. Yet on the basis of that simple decision, her life flowered as never before.

Before the rewards, however, was the commitment.

Before the blessings and bounty was the naked decision to follow the God of Israel...no matter where... no matter what.

It was springtime in Bethlehem. The time of

Passover. The beginning of barley harvest. In another day, another time, a royal descendant of Ruth would walk the same dusty roadways, look across the same field, and sing to his beloved…

"Rise up, my darling;
my fair one, come away.
For see, the winter is past!
The rains are over and gone;
the flowers appear in the countryside;
the season of birdsong is come,
and the turtle-dove's cooing is heard in our land;
the green figs ripen on the fig trees
and the vine blossoms give forth their fragrance.
Rise up, my darling;
my fair one, come away."[1]

Yet when Ruth the Moabitess went out that bright spring morning to glean in the barley fields, it's doubtful she had poetry on her mind. Gleaning, after all, was a matter of bare survival for her and her mother-in-law, and she didn't know what to expect or what she might face. Would she be well received in the fields? Would she be able to gather enough to keep them alive? Would the women be hostile? Would the men try to exploit her?

So many questions. Yet just as she had followed Naomi down a new path to a new country, so she courageously went off to find a field where she might labor.

She could not know, of course, that her late father-in-law had a wealthy kinsman named Boaz. The narrative tells us that "she happened to come to the part of the field belonging to Boaz, who was of the family of Elimelech" (2:3).

Neither she nor Naomi knew in whose field she would be gleaning. There was not scheming or planning. Yet even then, they were in the hands of the Sovereign One who does all things well. He was working His ways in and around and through their lives…in methods beyond their recognition, toward goals beyond their comprehension. And so He does with you and me.

When Ruth came home with her arms weighted with grain, her eyes full of wonder, and the name "Boaz" on her lips, Naomi immediately made the connection. You can almost see the older woman's eyes light up and hear strains of music in the background, *Matchmaker, matchmaker, make me a match…*" Shades of a loving Jewish mama laying wedding plans!

What Naomi actually said was "Blessed be he of the Lord, who has not forsaken His kindness to the living and the dead!… This man is a relative of ours, one of our near kinsmen" (2:20). The destitute women had found (and been found by) "a near kinsman."

♦♦♦

One quality in Ruth I admire very much was her refusal to "be cool" or "play it coy." You never find her pretending that Boaz's interest and kindness were of little consequence. In our day-to-day human interactions, we seem so prone to play little relational games and toy with one another's emotions. One of the favorite ploys, it seems, is slipping on that well-practiced mask of indifference and unruffled reserve in the presence of others.

For instance...if a fellow shows a little interest in a girl, she will often as not feign aloofness—even though inwardly she may delight in the attention. Delight, however, isn't "cool." And everyone knows it's a risk to appear "too interested."

Of course, this isn't uniquely a feminine trait. It's true of all human nature. At times each one of us prefers to be coy rather than frank and honest. We hesitate to make plain statements. We're reluctant to commit ourselves. It's a trait of our times. We don't want to appear too enthusiastic or excited about *anything*. Society's sophistry teaches, "Don't let anyone know what you're really feeling or thinking. It's so much safer to be neutral and noncommittal."

Ruth, however, was of a vastly different cut of cloth. And there is something about her spirit in this little book of Scripture that calls to mind my own courting experiences.

✦ ✦ ✦

I'll never forget when I first saw Anna.

Years ago—it amazes me to think how *many!*—I met my future wife on our college campus. I'd been at school the preceding year and returned after a summer away. My roommate and I (now sage and sophisticated sophomores) had just finished depositing our things in the dorm and were strolling across campus, speculating on what sort of year it might be.

My opinion on that subject was about to escalate dramatically.

We shortly encountered another group of students—some I knew, and some I didn't. And that's when I first saw her. She'd just come to school, and I met her during those moments when the eight or ten of us in that group stood talking and laughing together.

After a few minutes my friend and I said, "See you later," and continued on our way. But something had "clicked" when I met that girl. So it was that less than an hour into my first day back on campus, I had already made up my mind about one thing.

"Fred," I told my buddy, describing the new girl who had caught my eye, "I'm going to take that one out."

Did I take her out! Following our first date, about

ten days later, it wasn't two weeks before we were together all the time...from then on! But the pivotal moment was neither our first meeting nor that first date.
It was the Sunday *after* our first date. We attended the
same church—I played in the orchestra in the morning
worship, and she had joined the choir. That morning
our eyes met a couple of times during the service—she
in the choir loft and I in the orchestra pit—and we
smiled at each other. I thought to myself, *I'm going to
catch her right after church.*

Because I'd been around the previous year, I knew
where the choir left their robes. I could appear to be
"casually walking by" just as she walked out that door.
As a result of that cleverly arranged "chance meeting,"
we ended up having Sunday dinner together that day in
the dorm dining hall.

It wasn't particularly intimate or quiet—you know
what dormitory dining halls are like. What's more, following dinner I had an unglamorous role with the
clean-up crew. Several of us were "on duty" that week
with sponges, brooms, and mops.

So when we concluded our meal, I excused myself
and headed out to do my chores. I presumed she would
simply smile, take her leave, and return to her dorm and
her studies. After all, there was really no reason for her
to stay. We weren't going together or "serious," as we say,

so she certainly wasn't obliged to wait around for me to finish my "K.P." duty.

But she didn't leave.

Anna waited for me, she later explained, for the simple reason that I had walked with her to the dining hall. As she saw it, walking back with me was a matter of courtesy. There was nothing cloying, calculating, or possessive about her waiting. It was just plain thoughtfulness. So after clean-up that afternoon, I walked her back to her dorm. And that was that.

But to this day I remember being terrifically impressed, because most of the girls I'd known wouldn't have waited. They would have been embarrassed or worried about "how it looked," or concerned about appearing to "try too hard." They would have played it more cool, more reserved, more coy, more "cutesy."

But Anna's whole demeanor was different. Refreshingly so. I was impressed by the unaffectedness of that girl. There wasn't any pretense or game-playing about her. She was just herself. I liked that, and that was the reason I asked her for another date. Eventually, it was one of the main reasons I asked her to date me regularly...and then to marry me. Anna has always been like that. Sweet. Honest. Open. Steadfast. To me, her most endearing quality is her simple, unadorned sincerity. She's always the same. Even if she's irritated with me, she's still just herself, with no manipulating or maneuvering. In a world of three thousand exotic ice cream flavors, she is consistently and deliciously vanilla.

And I've always loved vanilla best of all.

+ + +

Qualities such as availability, simplicity, and unaffectedness are difficult to come by. It is fear that makes us pretend, masquerade, play our people games, or flirt with insincerity. To my way of thinking, Ruth depicts that same open-hearted quality I admire so much in my wife, Anna. It is a quality I think the Holy Spirit seeks to cultivate in all of us.

I believe He seeks honest hearts (2 Chronicles 16:9) and desires to help us discern those things that could keep us from finding the new time and place He has for each of us. He longs to deliver us from anything less than genuine or anything flavored by the cynical, ho-hum attitudes of our world's pseudosophistication.

Let the prophet's words stir you!

"Forget the former things;
do not dwell on the past.
See, I am doing a new thing!
Now it springs up; do you not perceive it?

I am making a way in the desert
and streams in the wasteland."
(Isaiah 43:18-19 NIV)

Let's all be done with the vain supposition we've "Mastered" anything. Let's refuse to entertain the notion that we "know all about this Christian life stuff" or that we've "heard it all before." We haven't! And even if we had, we need to hear it again and again! The Lord was telling his prophet, "Tell the people I want to do a *new* thing. Tell them neither to stagnate at former points of victory nor brood over past problems."

Permit me to ask you something rather pointedly: Are you prepared to allow the Spirit of God to change your status quo? Are you truly ready for the Lord to do something new in your life? Something unexpected? Out of the ordinary? Are you ready to follow Him down roads you've never traveled? Are you open to the possibility that He might bless you in an unexpected, perhaps startling way?

None of us would be so arrogant as to say, "I know it all," yet from time to time we may affect a certain blasé sophistication, a posture of pride that finds it stylish to be critical, cynical, or "laid back." Yet this prideful attitude *hamstrings* our ability to move into the fresh and the new…and grieves the Spirit of God.

Who says you know what's next for your life?

Who says God can't use you in a dramatic, wholly unexpected way?

Who says He can't lead you into a season of life and ministry beyond anything you've ever experienced—or even dreamed?

Just who is the limiting factor here? Is it God? Or are we capable of closing our hearts to what He wants to do in and through our lives?

Ruth is as simple and honest as a field lily, open-hearted as a child. It is a spiritual beauty we can all learn from. No wonder Boaz lost his heart in the barley field that spring morning!

Ruth had prepared herself to step out in faith and see what this God of Israel had to offer. As David would later put it, she was ready to "taste and see that the Lord is good" (Psalm 34:8). What a difference from the way Orpah responded back at the crossroads in Moab. That other daughter-in-law wept big tears, said all the right things, and even walked a few steps down the road with Naomi. But eventually she went back to what she knew. She turned back to her old relationships, her old haunts, her old expectations, and her old gods. As a result, she never found refuge under the wings of the eternal God, as Ruth did (2:12). She never tasted the sweet provision of the Lord in the land of promise.

✦ ✦ ✦

Scripture says Ruth "happened upon" the field of Boaz when the sun crept over the horizon that spring morning. A divine accident? Through the years I have discovered that when your heart is strongly inclined toward the Lord, He will see to it that your feet end up walking in the pathways and in the places that will accomplish His purposes in you.

So many people have sat with me in my office and moaned, "Oh…*if I could only* find the will of God! *If I could only* be sure of getting hold of His will!"

Yet the will of God is found in your heart.

You can get good counsel and read helpful books and diagram your life on the kitchen table, but ultimately, the answer is in your heart. And when your heart is totally given over to follow Christ and walk in His ways, you *can't miss* the will of God in the outworking of your daily life. He'll get your feet there, one way or another. Yes, the route may be roundabout. It might include a climb over some jagged mountains and dip down through some dry, rocky valleys. But He'll get you there.

I can't help but notice that Ruth found her way and her future in a harvest field. That's where things happen. That's where relationships develop and deepen and where destinies are revealed. True, none of us can *earn* a relationship with God by working for Him, but we can certainly *learn* the depths of such a relationship when we busy ourselves with what concerns Him most…*the harvest*.

To think of the biblical term "harvest" is to think of people *helping* people, *touching* people, *loving* people, *serving* people, and *winning* people into the love of God. On the other hand, to misplace or lose our perspective on "the harvest"—on serving people with *life*—is the surest way to short-circuit the promised possibilities of our lives.

I've found a common element in every individual who grows bitter, misses fulfillment, becomes sour, complains about God, falls into self-pity, or wonders "why nothing ever happens to me." That common denominator is a lost sense of *ministry*…of serving, loving, helping, and reaching out to men, women, and children in the Savior's name.

Ruth's life says to you and me: Get out into the harvest. Get out of yourself—touch lives for Jesus' sake. As you do, things will begin to happen. Without even being aware of it, you'll be edging ever nearer to that new time and place in your life.

✦ ✦ ✦

Naomi was a loving, concerned mother-in-law. Even though her own heart was broken with grief, she had deep concern for those young women who had married her sons. Back in Moab she had said to them: "The Lord grant that you may find rest, each in the house of her husband: (1:9). Later, after Boaz entered the picture, Naomi said to Ruth: "My daughter, shall I not seek security [or rest] for you, that it may be well with you?" (3:1).

When I entered into a relationship with Jesus Christ, I too discovered a wonderful gift of rest, just as He'd promised. He said:

"Come to Me, all you who labor and are heavy laden, and I will give you rest. Take My yoke upon you and learn from Me, for I am gentle and lowly in heart, and you will find rest for your souls."
(Matthew 11:28-29)

In other words, Jesus is saying, "If you really get involved with Me, and if you truly get into My work by My enabling power, you're going to discover a dimension of rest and relationship you never realized existed before."

The summons to us in the Word of God is so magnificent. Let's determine together to move toward a simple, humble relationship with our Savior, removed from sophistry or self-centeredness. Capitalize on the "Today" call of the Spirit (Psalm 95:7-8). To do so is to answer any questions that doubt or disbelief may pose.

"Just where is this new time and place?" we may ask ourselves. "Where is this place of abundance and rest?"

It's out there.

It's shaping itself right now on the horizon.

And the Lord is looking for open-hearted, obedient men and women who will stay in His field, walk in His way, and believe that, in Him, today can be dramatically different from yesterday.

I want to be one of them.

I'll bet you do, too.

---

[1] From The Song of Songs 2:10-13, Revised English Bible, © 1989 Oxford University Press and Cambridge University Press.

$\mathscr{A}$New Commitment

Then Naomi, her mother-in-law, said to her, "My daughter, shall I not seek security for you, that it may be well with you? Now Boaz, whose young women you were with, is he not our kinsman? In fact, he is winnowing barley tonight at the threshing floor. Therefore, wash yourself and anoint yourself, put on your best garment and go down to the threshing floor; but do not make yourself known to the man until he is finished eating and drinking. Then it shall be, when he lies down, that you shall notice the place where he lies; and you shall go in, uncover his feet, and lie down; and he will tell you what you should do." And she said to her, "All that you say to me I will do."

So she went down to the threshing floor and did according to all that her mother-in-law instructed her. After Boaz had eaten and drunk, and his heart was cheerful, he went to lie down at the end of the heap of grain; and she came softly, uncovered his feet, and lay down.

Now it happened at midnight that the man was startled,

and turned himself; and there, a woman was lying at his feet. And he said, "Who are you?" So she answered, "I am Ruth, your maidservant. Take your maidservant under your wing, for you are a near kinsman." Then he said, "Blessed are you of the Lord, my daughter! For you have shown more kindness at the end than at the beginning, in that you did not go after young men, whether poor or rich. And now, my daughter, do not fear. I will do for you all that you request, for all the people of my town know that you are a virtuous woman. Now it is true, I am your near kinsman; however, there is a kinsman nearer than I. Stay this night, and in the morning it shall be that if he will perform the duty of a near kinsman for you—good; let him do it. But if he does not want to perform the duty for you, then I will perform the duty for you, as the Lord lives! Lie down until morning."

So she lay at his feet until morning, and she arose before one could recognize another. Then he said, "Do not let it be known that the woman came to the threshing floor." Also he said, "Bring the shawl that is on you and hold it." And when she held it, he measured six ephahs of barley and laid it on her. Then she went into the city.

When she came to her mother-in-law, she said, "Is that you, my daughter?" Then she told her all that the man had done for her. And she said, "These six ephahs of barley he gave me; for he said to me, 'Do not go empty-handed to your mother-in-law'" Then she said, "Sit still, my daughter, until *you know how the matter will turn out; for the man will not rest until he has concluded the matter this day." (Ruth 3)*

$\mathcal{A}$ NEW COMMITMENT

All of us know what it means to lose.

In one form or another, we have all tasted the bitterness of loss. We have all held the ashes of once-lovely dreams and felt them slip through our fingers.

We may lose through circumstances over which we have no control. We may lose by simply being in the wrong place at the wrong time. We may lose through our own carelessness, mismanagement, or ignorance. We may lose, as Elimelech lost, because of a faithless decision that changes the entire course of our lives.

People in days of the Old Testament were no different. Some suffered loss through no fault of their own. Others tasted failure and loss because of their foolishness or deliberate sin.

But in those days, about the worst thing you could lose was your inheritance.

In Israel, God intended that everyone would have a family inheritance of property. A place to live. A parcel of earth on which to pitch a tent. A piece of land for raising crops or livestock. A little corner of the world where a person might provide for his family and watch his children play tag in the sun. The land might have a shack on it, or it might have a mansion; it might be well favored and well watered, or it might be a pile of rocks and nettles. Nevertheless, it was to be his. Something he could call his own, and something he could leave for his descendants.

This was as God intended and prescribed. When His people came into Canaan after generations of slavery in Egypt, He also prescribed the national boundaries. Within those boundaries, He established tribal boundaries. And within the tribal designations, each family got its own piece of the promised land.

But as we said, people lose things.

Even their most precious possessions.

Even their family inheritance.

Yet God in His grace foresaw that possibility, too. In His plan, death and loss would not have the final word. What was lost might be redeemed.

All it would require was a redeemer.

◆ ◆ ◆

Ruth had entered a new time and a new place. She had begun to experience new provision, drinking the wine and tasting the bread of her adopted land. And not so very long after that, she faced an invitation to a new commitment.

In Boaz, she would find that close relative, in God's order and providence, would become her "redeemer"— her *kinsman-redeemer*. This term lies at the heart of the book of Ruth…and needs a little explaining. The Old Testament books of Leviticus and Deuteronomy provide the source material for a deeper understanding.

If ever a family's property was lost—through tragedy, poor business management, or for whatever reason—those boundaries and that inheritance could be reinstated to the family through the action of a near relative. In Hebrew, that relative or "kinsman" was called the *goel*, or the "kinsman-redeemer."

In literal terms, *goel* means "he who establishes or reestablishes a claim; the one who enforces it." So the recovery of a lost inheritance could be realized through the enforcement of a prior claim, but only if someone could and would step into the situation as a willing and qualified redeemer.

What kind of "someone"?

Someone who would care about what was lost.

Someone who would do something about it.

Someone who would pay the price of redemption.

Sometimes the role of kinsman-redeemer went beyond financial obligations. If the situation called for it, there was yet another demanding responsibility to be performed. A person's loss of real estate was one thing, but what if there was no *heir*? What if the rightful heir was lost or dead? Who would inherit the property even if it was retained? Who would hold it and manage it in the name of the deceased?

That was precisely the situation of Ruth and Naomi. The family property had been lost through the deaths of Elimelech, Mahlon, and Chilion, and even if the property could be restored, there were no male heirs to see that the inheritance was held and cared for.

It was for just such a dilemma that God had established an additional provision. To our way of thinking, this added provision might seem strange. Bizarre. Even shocking. Yet God always has good reasons for whatever He decrees—no matter how it strikes our modern sensibilities.

So it was, under the old covenant, that the kinsman-redeemer would not only provide for the *financial* reinstatement of a widow's property, but he would also take on the *biological* responsibility of providing her with an heir to inherit and manage that property. Deuteronomy 25:5-10 reveals how God offered a way for a family to recover from an otherwise irredeemable loss. But that recovery could only be assured through the self-sacrifice of a near relative who would take the widow into his own household and receive her in his family as an added wife. He would father children by her and raise and care for those children—even though they would never be reckoned as his own. The children would be named and regarded as the dead relative's family and would become heir to the dead man's restored property and inheritance.

Why did God make such a provision?

There were a number of reasons, but one that might be overlooked is the simple fact that He has shown through *all* His Word that He cares deeply about the plight of widows—often the most vulnerable members of any society. And since there was no such thing as welfare or Social Security or food stamps—or even the living church of our Lord Jesus Christ—this was part of His gracious plan to meet desperate needs.

Conditioned as we may be by this sensual, lurid culture in which we live, this "additional wife" arrangement might sound a little racy or risqué. Yet it was not an arrangement driven by lust or passion. It was a duty God assigned seriously, a vital social welfare plan to be sure—but *more*. It was also a means through which He revealed His own very nature as *redeemer*.

✦ ✦ ✦

It is a constant in God's economy: That which is lost may be reinstated, that which is wasted may be recovered, and that which is lost may be restored!

Above all expressions of His love, God, at His heart, is a Redeemer...a Reclaimer, a Restorer, a Reviver, a Reinstator! He illustrated it in this policy of His under the old covenant, in the way a kinsman-redeemer would restore lost property. But He revealed even more. In the way that "seed" could be raised up in place of a dead father, God was revealing in advance His plan to restore with the grandest of all dimensions—*resurrection!* He is able to bring dead things to life and wasted things back to reinstatement. That message is woven throughout the Bible, and it finds beautiful, powerful illustration in the story of Naomi, Ruth, and Boaz.

Hear me in this, friend: *It is not the will of God that anybody, for whatever reason, live out his or her life as a loser.* None of us are ever in a situation beyond His ability to redeem. If He could take a stranger and foreigner and bring her into the ancestry of kings through a kinsman-redeemer, He can also say to you and me, "Whatever distance you may be from where you ought to be and where I would like you to be, I can cause the purpose I have *for* you to be realized *in* you."

The Philippians letter says it all:

He who began a good work in you will complete it. …
For it is God who works in you both to will and to do for
His good pleasure.

(Philippians 1:6; 2:13)

✦ ✦ ✦

No matter how you read Ruth chapter 3, most of us wrestle with what on the surface seems like questionable counsel from a manipulative older woman. It's all too easy to imagine Naomi saying, "Listen up, Honey. Here's how to snag a man. Put on a dab of Chanel No. 5 behind each ear, slip on a slinky outfit, and go and wait 'til he's full of wine. Watch where he lies down to sleep, then, after dark, sneak over there, pull the covers back, and crawl in beside him. When he wakes up, say, 'What do you want me to do?'"

My sincere apologies if you've never entertained such a thought. I salute your apparent naiveté. But most people I know struggle just a bit with Naomi's counsel. Our struggle, however, is born of a thinness in our understanding of that culture, not to mention a thickness in our souls from the hardening effect of a world that has lost its innocence.

The pure facts, tied to the times of which we read, actually address our two most dubious questions: "Why this counsel, Naomi?" and "What did you *really* mean?"

First, why did Naomi direct Ruth to go *at night* to speak to Boaz, out on the threshing floor? The simple truth is, she came at night in order to avoid embarrassing the esteemed and respected farmer. In that culture, it would have been highly inappropriate for Ruth to approach Boaz at his house or in the field in broad daylight. It would have appeared pushy and presumptuous …a brazen, unseemly thing for a woman of that time to do. It certainly would not have earned the man's praise or respect.

Second, what did Naomi have in mind when she told Ruth to say, "Take your maidservant under your wing"? Was this some sort of seductive suggestion? Not at all. On the contrary, the literal Hebrew rendering reads: "Stretch forth the mantle or the border of your garment over me." Boaz could not have mistaken Ruth's intent. He knew exactly what she was asking, and it was, in essence: "I'm asking you to exercise your office of kinsman-redeemer and be a covering and a protection for me. According to the word of the Lord God, you are the person in position to redeem or reclaim my circumstance and that of Naomi. Whatever promise or hope we have lies with you, and it is to you we make our appeal."

There wasn't a hint of impurity in Ruth's words or actions. Boaz knew very well what her approach meant, as evidence by his reply. Boaz's words in verse 11, "you are a virtuous woman," make it clear that he believed her to be highly moral—and her request perfectly appropriate.

Wrapped up in Ruth's request, however, was another deeply personal request, and it must have been humbling for the young woman to speak. But because there was no one to speak for her, Ruth looked up in the darkness at the silhouette of Boaz and said the words herself. And Boaz rightly understood her to be saying, *"Will you take me into your home as a wife?"*

Boaz was unmarried and older than Ruth, yet his response had nothing to do with passion or lust. Marriages in that day were arranged and were not based— at least initially—on mutual physical attraction.

Yet there can be no doubt the man was moved. Here was a lovely, gracious, young woman lying at his feet in the starlight, appealing for his protection and provision. He recognized her as a woman who had made honorable, selfless choices, beginning at the bleak crossroads in Moab. And now here she was—a foreigner and alien— laying hold of a provision in the law of Israel's God.

If you had been Boaz, you would have probably said just what he said that night. *"The Lord bless you!"* A paraphrase of his remarks might read something like this: "Lady, you're so attractive and charming that you could have gone after any eligible bachelor you wanted to, and there are certainly men who are younger and wealthier than I am. But instead, you have taken the course of the Lord's covenant provision for a redeemer. Rather than making your own best arrangements, you've chosen the path of God's Word and God's way. May He bless you, dear woman!"

Ruth could have checked out all the possibilities around Bethlehem. In fact, out there in the field, she would have met plenty of prospects. But that was not her course, and Boaz blessed her name for that. There is a tender beauty in his response as he honors her for the purity of her quest and acknowledges his willingness to exercise the office of kinsman-redeemer.

Before he made any promises, however, he raised an issue we'll look at in the next chapter. He said to her, "You couldn't have known it, but there is a kinsman nearer than I, and in the order of God, we must first check with him before I can exercise the duty of near kinsman."

In that response, Boaz revealed the purity of his own motivations. He went on to say:

"Stay this night, and in the morning it shall be that if he will perform the duty of a near kinsman for you—good; let him do it. But if he does not want to perform the duty

for you, then I will perform the duty for you, as the Lord lives!" (Ruth 3:13)

These words show a genuine heart interest in the woman and her circumstances, and not in what he might have done to exploit or take advantage of her. There's a beauty in this, as he says to her, "I'll take care of it in the morning. Now you stay here for tonight." And Scripture tells us that "She lay at his feet until morning" (3:14).

There is a sound reason why Boaz invited Ruth to stay that night. He had reason to be concerned for the young woman's safety. It was now late at night, and in those days lions prowled the hills and valleys of Judah. But even more dangerous during those turbulent, lawless days of the judges were the *two-legged* predators who also stalked the night.

Boaz told her, "You stay right here, and I'll keep you safe until morning. Then I will do all I can to see to your redemption."

She rose before dawn to return home, but she didn't go empty-handed. He first poured six measures of barley into her shawl. This action was his means of confirming to Naomi, via Ruth, that he was establishing a pledge. He was taking her appeal seriously and would do all that was in his power to help and redeem.

Message sent. Message received.

Naomi was understandably thrilled with this turn of events. She told Ruth:

"Sit still, my daughter, until you know how the matter will turn out; for the man will not rest until he has concluded the matter this day." (3:18)

✦ ✦ ✦

"All that you say to me," Ruth had told Naomi, "I will do."

Ruth realized when she went to the threshing floor that night that she was making herself vulnerable to serious misunderstanding. This step toward commitment was not without its risks. Yet Ruth had already made her choice back in Moab. She was already walking the pathway of faith, and she would heed and follow this course as far in God's grace as it might lead.

At this point of vulnerability in Ruth's story, we see the story of every believer's life. Our commitment to follow the Lord Jesus and the life of faith will not always win the love or respect of a self-serving society.

We can be ever so careful to walk uprightly, hold forth our light, and contribute a tang of preserving salt—becoming the very fragrance of life in the midst of a decaying society (Philippians 2:14-15). Yet Jesus Himself tells us we must expect rejection and hatred from the world at large (see John 15:20; 16:1-4). Even so, dear one, that fact never gives us license to offend the world by obnoxious behavior or a pompous attitude. While Jesus warns us specifically that the world will love only its own, that doesn't mean we should "lead with our chin" and deliberately seek to be misunderstood. We must not wrap our insensitivity or lack of courtesy in a "holy robe" by saying, "They just don't understand. I'm living for Jesus!" That kind of spiritual snobbery isn't worth a snap of the fingers on God's scale. But misunderstanding is something we can expect as a matter of course. It should never take us by surprise.

In a recent study of John's gospel I was struck anew by what must have been a stinging incident in Jesus' life. One day in the temple He was in an intense conversation with the Jews. He was about to make the point that though they claimed Abraham as their father, their true father was the devil, because their hearts were full of murder and deceit.

Before He made that point, however, the Jews threw what appears to be a nasty insinuation at Him. Can you hear the *sneer* in the following words?

Then they said to Him, "We were not born of fornication; we have one Father—God." (John 8:41)

In essence, they were saying to Jesus, "*We're* not the ones born of fornication. *We're* not bastard children." Most likely, they referred to a shadow lingering over the circumstances of Jesus' supernatural birth. It was apparently whispered that there had been "something unusual" about His conception and parentage. Those insinuations followed Him through the years, from Nazareth all the way to Jerusalem.

A look at the life of Mary teaches us how association with Jesus often brings the scorn of the world. Mary clearly lived out her life knowing her Son's paternity was in question. She suffered that indignity of doubt and criticism because of one unforgettable day when an angel visited her and said, in effect, "Mary, you are to become a channel for the flow of God's life into the world." And notwithstanding the possibility of misunderstanding, she said, "Behold the maidservant of the Lord! Let it be to me according to your word" (Luke 1:38).

That was Ruth's heart, too.

Come what may, in spite of whatever misunderstanding or complications might result, Ruth said, "All that you say I will do."

On another day, in Cana of Galilee, Jesus was giving strange instructions to several servants concerning six large, stone water jars. At this point, no one had seen Him perform a miracle. No one imagined what He might do next. Not even Mary knew what He intended to do. But she *did* know what to say in that moment.

His mother said to the servants, "Whatever He says to

you, do it." (John 2:5)

In other words, "No matter what this Man asks you to do, no matter how strange or unusual it might seem, just go ahead and do it. Do it just as He says."

Listen to these three replies once again…

"All that you say to me I will do."

"Let it be to me according to your word."

"Whatever He says to you, do it."

What are we talking about here? We're talking about the kind of commitment that opens the way for the kingly purposes of the living God to be realized in and through us.

The kingdom happens through people who heed the Word and the counsel of the Lord. And these are the people who find the dimensions and delights of the new time and the new place God longs for each one of us to have.

What Naomi told Ruth to do was straight out of Scripture. It wasn't some manipulative device to snag a rich husband for a former daughter-in-law. She knew in her heart that "this is the way we can appropriately and graciously approach this subject that God has ordained in His Word."

People who move into a new commitment through obedience to the Word of God find themselves experiencing recovery, renewal, reconstruction, redevelopment, and resurrection power in and through their lives.

All of us who know the Lord hunger to be used and filled and empowered in such a way, and the qualifications for us are no different than the qualification for Ruth.

"All that you say to me I will do."

✦ ✦ ✦

Now it happened at midnight that the man was startled, and turned himself; and there, a woman was lying at his feet. (Ruth 3:8)

Finally, in her quest for a redeemer, Ruth came to his feet.

She had first come into Boaz's *land* in the wake of a tragedy. Then she came into his *fields* in the heat of the day. Now, she was *at his feet* in the middle of the night.

In application, this speaks to me of those who steadily progress in to the circle of Jesus' influence.

They come into "His land," so to speak, seeking *refuge.*

Then they come into "His fields," seeking *supply.*

Then, finally, there are those who fall down at His feet, *seeking relationship* and all that He has for them.

Boaz awoke in the night, discovered Ruth, heard her request, and made a commitment to her. "I'll take care of this in the morning," he told her. "You stay right here until then." And the text says she "lay at his feet until morning."

Each one of us has faced very real, very long nights of the soul. Times when everything seems dark and cold and hopeless. And many of us have come to *the* great Redeemer in those long nights. We've thrown ourselves at His feet and said, "Lord, I'm looking for Your answer. Redeem. Help me." And He has said, "I will do that which you ask. Stay near Me through this night, and I'll attend to it in the morning."

Ruth stayed. And in the first light of dawn, there was provision. Before that day was through, there was complete redemption. Tragically, however, the trait of all too many of us is to ask for our Lord's help in the darkness, only to get up and leave before He replies! When we don't get an immediate answer, we leave His feet and stumble on through the darkness, trying to work it out on our own. Yet our Lord is saying to us, "If you'll just stay at My feet, I'll handle it by My hands, not yours. I'll settle it in My time, not yours. You come and stay at My feet and enjoy My nearness and protection. There are dangers in the darkness—stay beside me."

Not long ago, a young man in our fellowship was going through a season of deep emotional darkness. But he refused to wait at Jesus' feet. He refused to wait for the morning light and the Lord's redemption and, in a moment of despair, took his own life. How I ache over the loss! Obviously, that was an extreme situation, but it happens in a thousand other ways when we refuse to wait on the Lord and instead choose to take matters into our hands. Please hear this: *There is no night so long or so dark but if you stay at the feet of the Lord, He will take care of it in the morning. But we need to learn to come and wait at the Redeemer's feet.*

People may learn how to pray and how to praise. People may come into the assembly of believers and lift their hands and glorify the Lord and sing a thousand songs. Yet these things will never substitute for those long hours at the feet of Jesus—often spent "in the dark"—either of night or of circumstance. And those who have learned to live at His feet, clinging to His promises and waiting on Him, experience a dimension of life and fruitfulness beyond what they have ever known before.

One more thing...

Ruth came to the threshing floor at the end of the barley harvest. In ancient Israel, as today, the barley harvest began at Passover, continued through Pentecost, and climaxed with the feast of first fruits. In that light, the New Testament outpouring of the Holy Spirit at Pentecost—during the celebration of the "first fruits"—takes on added meaning. For just as those who stay at Jesus' feet will discover His sustaining presence through dark nights, so will they also discover fresh outpourings of the Holy Spirit upon their lives. And just as Boaz filled Ruth's apron with grain as a pledge of his firm intent, so the Word declares those Holy Spirit workings as a "down payment" on the great inheritance that's ahead for us (see Romans 8:23 and Ephesians 1:13-14).

When Ruth walked away from Boaz and the threshing floor in the dim light of that early morning, she walked away alone. Yet she walked away with his firm promise and a "down payment" of grain, a foretaste of the great provision to come.

For a brief time, she couldn't see him, couldn't hear his voice, and couldn't feel the touch of his strong, gentle hand on her shoulder. It was probably a very long day for Ruth. Yet Naomi told her, "Sit still, my daughter…for the man will not rest until he has concluded the matter this day" (3:18).

Similarly, for you and me there will be times when we may feel the Savior is a million miles away from our situation. But receive the promise, dear one. He has placed His Spirit within you and me as a certified assurance of His will to *complete everything!* And until He settles all things and eventually takes us home to Himself, we may continually rely on the presence of the living God. No matter how dark or long your night, He has pledged, "I will never leave you nor forsake you!"

So come and bow again. At this very moment, affirm your commitment to wait before His throne—dependent on His presence, His power, and His promise.

Jesus, according to Your Word, I will wait at Your feet, for You ARE my Redeemer. However dark or long the night, I receive Your provision, and I commit to live in the inheritance of the Holy Spirit You have given unto me...en route to the fullness of Your purpose in my new time and new place.

Chapter Four

A Redeemer Steps In

Now Boaz went up to the gate and sat down there; and behold, the near kinsman of whom Boaz had spoken came by.
So Boaz said, "Come aside, friend, sit down here." So he
came aside and sat down. And he took ten men of the elders
of the city, and said, "Sit down here." So they sat down. Then
he said to the near kinsman, "Naomi, who has come back
from the country of Moab, sold the piece of land which be-
longed to our brother Elimelech. And I thought to inform
you, saying, 'Buy it back in the presence of the inhabitants
and the elders of my people. If you will redeem it, redeem it;
but if you will not redeem it, then tell me that I may know;
for there is no one but you to redeem it, and I am next after
you.'" And he said, "I will redeem it." Then Boaz said, "On
the day you buy the field from the hand of Naomi, you must
also buy it from Ruth the Moabitess, the wife of the dead, to
perpetuate the name of the dead through his inheritance."
And the near kinsman said, I cannot redeem it for myself,
lest I ruin my own inheritance. You redeem my right of re-

demption for yourself, for I cannot redeem it."

Now this was the custom in former times in Israel concerning redeeming and exchanging, to confirm anything: one man took off his sandal and gave it to the other, and this was an attestation in Israel. Therefore the near kinsman said to Boaz, "Buy it for yourself." So he took off his sandal. And Boaz said to the elders and to all the people, "You are witnesses this day that I have bought all that was Elimelech's, and all that was Chilion's and Mahlon's, from the hand of Naomi. Moreover, Ruth the Moabitess, the widow of Mahlon, I have acquired as my wife, to perpetuate the name of the dead through his inheritance, that the name of the dead may not be cut off from among his brethren and from his position at the gate. You are witnesses this day." And all the people who were at the gate, and the elders said, "We are witnesses." (Ruth 4:1-11a)

$\mathcal{A}$ REDEEMER STEPS IN

It was one o'clock in the morning, and I was too tired to sleep. I had arrived back home after a speaking trip of several days in another part of the country. I greeted Anna, we talked a bit, and then she went on to bed. I felt such a profound weariness I wanted just to sit quietly in the living room for a few minutes and collect myself before I joined her.

Something more than physical exhaustion pressed me down in the easy chair that night years ago. For several weeks I had experienced the push and pull of what seemed like a thousand demands. I felt distraught and uncertain—nerves stretched thin by stress. More than this, I didn't know what to do about it! I didn't see any relief ahead or any escape from the treadmill that was running me into tatters. And I was tired—so terribly tired—of trying to work it all out in my own strength.

As I sat in that chair, I knew there had to be an answer that I couldn't find on my own. I sensed something missing in my spirit. The recollection of that moment is as clear as any memory in my life. I remember looking in the soft lamplight across the living room at the open doorway that led into the hall.

Exhausted, choked up, and at my wit's end, I said right out loud, *"Jesus, I wish You'd walk through that door right now and tell me what I'm supposed to do!"*

The funny thing is, I meant it. It was a real prayer. That's how desperate I was. I can't remember uttering anything like that before or since, but at that moment it was the very cry of my heart.

Now...what if He had literally answered my prayer? What if He had chosen to walk bodily through the doorway into my living room that night?

I don't know about you, but I doubt very much I would have stood up and said, "Well, how nice! Pull up a chair. Would you enjoy a cup of coffee?" No, I immediately would have had a face full of carpet. If I could have even remained conscious, I would have made myself as flat as a throw rug.

Yet I was desolate enough to ask for that very thing.

As it turned out, He didn't step through the doorway that night. I can't say I really *expected* Him to, because that's not the way the Lord usually answers such prayers.

I didn't feel disappointed, let down, or neglected. I just felt the same as I had before I spoke the prayer. Heavy. Worried. Bone tired. Desperately desiring His intervention in my life.

I went to bed, rolled out at the usual time in the morning, and dressed. Driving in to work, I felt as tired as I had the previous night. Confusion and uncertainly weighted down my shoulders like an overloaded packboard.

Walking into my office, I immediately saw a note on my desk. It was from Darryl, a dear friend and a member of our pastoral staff. I was a little surprised. Darryl isn't the note-writing type. I sat down and began to read:

Jack, I was praying for you the other day while you were out of town. And the Lord impressed me with something I need to say to you...

What followed were some rather specific directions, composed in Darryl's quiet, respectful way, regarding several major situations I was facing. And as I read, I suddenly knew very clearly in my heart that it was Jesus speaking to me.

I continued to read in the early-morning quiet. My secretary hadn't even arrived yet. Before I could finish the note, however, a timid knock drew my attention to the open door. I looked up to see the wife of one of our elders standing in the doorway.

"Pastor," she said, "may I speak with you a minute?"

"Of course. Come on in. Won't you sit down?"

She came over and instead stood beside my desk.

"I really can't stay more than a minute," she said. "I've got to run to an appointment. But as I was praying this morning, I felt the Lord leading me to stop by— and say something to you. Pastor, I really have no idea how this is going to sound to you..."

She began to tell me what was on her heart, and it was virtually the same message contained in my half-read note from Darryl! I listened to her without interrupting, and when she was done, I said, "You have no idea how that speaks to my heart. Thank you so much." She smiled, relieved to have delivered her message, and was on her way.

The lady had hardly walked out the door when my secretary stepped into the outer office. She knew nothing of Darryl's note, nor of the woman's words to me that morning. But as she was hanging up her sweater and getting her desk organized for the day, she said, "Pastor, before we get started, I wonder if I might speak to you."

She began talking to me about something the Lord had said to her, and in her own way, she echoed the counsel of Darryl and the elder's wife. By that time, I was leaning back in my chair thinking, *Oh Lord Jesus, You really do love me!*

It didn't stop there. When the mail came, I opened a letter that essentially repeated the same refrain I'd already heard three times that day—and the letter had been written four days earlier. In the afternoon, another friend dropped by, saying, "You know, I just wanted to come and pray with you because the Lord has put something very specific on my heart concerning you." Each individual had a slightly different angle on the same issue, but it was all distilling into a major sense of a fresh direction in my life.

I went home thinking what a day it had been! I was feeling better...lighter...as though a load had already slipped from my shoulders. Around nine-thirty that evening, I found myself in the same living-room chair I'd been sitting in about twenty hours earlier.

The phone rang. My dad was calling from Oakland.

"Son," he said, "this is really different for me. As long as I've been filled with the Spirit and walked in the life of Jesus, I've never had a word from the Lord to give *anybody*. But He's given me a word for you tonight. I want to deliver that now."

What Dad began to tell me was actually a summary of what I'd been hearing all day long. By that time, I was nearly a basket case. I couldn't stop the tears. But my dad wasn't done.

"Now, Son," he said, "before I hang up, I feel like

I'm supposed to anoint you with oil. But here I am in Oakland! Would you go into the kitchen and get some olive oil and come back?"

I came back to the phone with the oil. "Son, this may sound strange to you," my father said, "but I don't think you're supposed to anoint yourself as we usually do—putting a little on the forehead. I want you to take the bottle and pour it out over your head. Will you do that, Son?"

I did.

So there I sat, in the same chair as the night before, my head dripping with oil, my eyes overflowing with tears, and my daddy on the phone in Oakland praying his heart out for me. When I finally hung up the phone, rubbing back the tears and the oil, I looked over at the doorway I'd stared at the night before—and my heart almost broke for joy.

"Jesus, You did it!" I said. *"You did it!"*

He had stepped through the door of my life and told me what I was supposed to do. He had placed His message in the mouths of a number of witnesses and then—not content with that—anointed me with oil, bringing healing to my anxious, troubled soul and consecrating me afresh to His service.

What a Lord! What a Redeemer!

It was one of the most important "hinge" moments

in my life and ministry, because of a decision I made at the pivotal time. I had been doing everything I knew to do to accomplish what I thought God wanted me to accomplish. And it was wearing me to a frazzle.

Then the Lord stepped in.

Through that series of events, I heard Him saying to me, "Son, I never intended you to accomplish this task on your own. Will you let Me handle this now?" That day began a dismantling of the frantic activity I'd been caught up in without even realizing it.

I could sing with David,

My eyes are ever toward the Lord,
For He shall pluck my feet out of the net.
(Psalm 25:15)

Yes, I had known very well that salvation and the flow of God's life through us are by grace and not by works. I had long understood that the power to achieve the Lord's work in men and women's lives was essentially His. But somehow…I'd become caught in the iron teeth of a "performance" trap. And it was bleeding me dry.

Jesus heard my cry that night, stepped through the door, released me from the snare, and met me in my weakness.

It is His specialty.

Redemption and deliverance aren't something we do

for ourselves. The Book of Ruth, through a series of unforgettable pictures, paints a lovely mural of *dependence* upon the Lord...and what results from such dependence. In case any of us has forgotten—or perhaps never known—we need to see again what happens when the Redeemer steps in.

◆ ◆ ◆

Ruth chapter four is alive with redemptive activity.

But Ruth wasn't involved in any of it.

She wasn't even present at the scene.

When Boaz went to the gate of the city, gathered witnesses, assembled the elders, spoke to the nearer kinsman, and completed the entire transaction, Ruth the Moabitess wasn't anywhere near. Though her destiny hung in the balance, she was at home with Naomi. While she quietly waited, redemption was accomplished by another.

I hear a simple message in that fact: God doesn't need my help to redeem my situation. As a matter of fact, the more I try to "help," the more I get in the way.

Naomi had told her daughter-in-law, "*Sit still*, my daughter, until you know how the matter will turn out; for the man will not rest until he has concluded the matter this day" (3:18).

It's ludicrous, but for a moment try to imagine Ruth saying to herself, *I'd better make sure Boaz really follows through. Men are so easily distracted. I'll just wander down to the city gate today and look around a bit. I need to do a little shopping anyway. I'll stand over to one side and watch the proceedings—just to make sure this thing's in motion.*

So in this little imaginary scenario, Boaz stands up and says, "My brothers, we need ten elders to complete this transaction, and we've only got seven so far."

Ruth, over to one side, thinks, *I knew I could help out.* She pipes up and says, "Excuse me. I hate to interrupt, but I know where a couple of these fellows live. I could run down the street and knock on a few doors. It would only take a minute. We'll have those elders gathered in no time. And then we can start assembling the witnesses. I've got a few ideas about how we might round 'em up. I've been thinking about it. I can help. I've just got to do *something.*"

It's ridiculous, isn't it? But let's allow our imaginations to run a bit further. Imagine that Boaz begins his presentation and says to that nearer kinsman, "If you will redeem it, go ahead and redeem it." But there's Ruth standing at the edge of the group waving frantically and saying in a stage whisper, "Pssst. Boaz! I don't *want* him to redeem me! I don't *want* it to turn out that way. Please don't give him that much of a chance!"

Thankfully, Scripture gives us a different story. After Ruth made her appeal according to the provisions of God's Word, she stepped back. In quiet dignity, she let the redeemer redeem. She left it in the hands of Boaz...and God. As difficult as it may have been, she obeyed Naomi's counsel to "sit still" until the matter was concluded one way or another.

But "sitting still" isn't the easiest thing to do, is it? Something about our flesh yearns to "help God out a little."

The truth is, we could never have found salvation at all if we had insisted on adding our own good works and worthy deeds to our redemption price. It would have been an abomination! What could we possibly add to the price Jesus paid on the cross? Nothing, nothing, nothing!

Yet we seem to feel that once we've been ushered into His Kingdom by grace, we must somehow "make the kingdom happen" through the frenzied energy of our flesh. And when we get ourselves into trouble and paint ourselves into impossible corners, we imagine that we can somehow ("just this time") help the Redeemer redeem us.

Paul saw that very attitude cropping up among the believers in Galatia, prompting him to write (with some heat):

Are you so foolish? Having begun in the Spirit, are you now being made perfect by the flesh? (Galatians 3:3)

Like Ruth, we are privileged to answer the Spirit's call to depend totally—*totally*—upon our Redeemer. As Jesus said, "It is the Spirit who gives life; the flesh profits nothing" (John 6:63). Ruth's absence in the redemptive activity and Boaz's capacity to handle it completely and thoroughly is a message we need to ponder.

There are times in life when the very best thing we can do is to "sit still"…and let the Redeemer redeem.

✦ ✦ ✦

Strictly speaking, it was not in Boaz's best interest to redeem.

To begin with, he risked what must have been a sterling reputation in the community. Marrying a young foreign woman might have raised some eyebrows in Bethlehem.

Thankfully, in our culture most interracial marriages no longer carry the stigma they once did. Yet in Israel at that time, there were good reasons for this stigma. Throughout much of the nation's history, the Lord had warned His people against intermarrying with their neighbors, lest they begin to worship foreign gods and adopt destructive pagan ways. Ruth the Moabitess had clearly embraced the living God of Israel. Even so, her Moabitish origin might well have made her suspect. And the fact that this upstart foreigner had landed one of the more eligible bachelors in town couldn't have helped her popularity.

Yet Boaz laid down his reputation when he chose to act as kinsman-redeemer. Ruth may have been a lovely young woman, but he did not act in self-interest.

Nor did Boaz have anything to gain financially by redeeming the property of his dead relative. Already a prosperous man, he didn't need Elimelech's estate at all. We have seen that he had plenty of work and a thriving farm.

Why did he do it? Why did he risk his reputation and resources? For the simple reason that it was in the heart of this good man to redeem! And how wonderful the precision of the analogy, for in the same way, the living God doesn't need "more to do." After all, He has a universe to administer. He has places to go and things to do. He has legions of angels flashing through the cosmos at the speed of thought, doing His bidding on missions our minds can't even conceive. But wonder of wonders, He not only stepped down to our dust-speck planet to save us from our sins and the sentence of death, He *continually* steps into our lives as Redeemer. He continues to hear and respond when we cry out to Him from the quicksand of our circumstances. He redeems because it is in the great heart of God to redeem.

When Jesus came to earth, He came at unimaginable expense to Himself. Do you remember the hymn Christians of past generations used to sing?

Out of the ivory palaces, into a world of woe,

Only His great redeeming love, made my Savior go.

Ivory palaces or not, our minds are simply incapable of visualizing the radiant splendor and glory from which He turned away. Our thoughts are not wired to imagine the majesty and beauty He set aside.

As clearly as inspired human language can serve, Philippians chapter two describes His great descent. Jesus knew He was God, knew He possessed the infinite resources of heaven at His fingertips. But He laid it all down. He *emptied* Himself. He made Himself of "no reputation." When He stepped into human flesh, He poured out all of His prerogatives as God, choosing to be completely and totally *human.*

None of the things you see Jesus doing in His life are a result of His functioning as God, the Second Person of the Trinity. Instead, He chose to function as a Holy-Spirit-enabled human being. He came on human terms. He lived and suffered and died in a normal human body.

Why did He do that?

He did it so He might become our near kinsman. Our

goel. Our kinsman-redeemer. He chose to be our close relative.

Listen to the Book of Hebrews:

Since the children [that's us] have flesh and blood, He too shared in their humanity so that by His death He might destroy him who holds the power of death—that is, the devil—and free those who all their lives were held in slavery by their fear of death…. For this reason He had to be made like His brothers in every way, in order that He might become a merciful and faithful high priest in service to God, and that He might make atonement for the sins of the people.

(Hebrews 2:14-15, 17 NIV)

He became human so that He might redeem. He stepped out of eternity and into time so that He might rescue us from slavery and restore us to our lost estate and adopt us into the royal family of heaven. All of that. For you and me.

Hold that thought in your heart very long, and you'll be face down on the ground along with Ruth, saying, "Why have I found favor in your eyes, that you should take notice of me, since I am a foreigner?" (Ruth 2:10).

He came because it was the only way. Only a near kinsman could have redeemed us. He wasn't our kinsman as God, because that relationship had been shattered by Adam's sin. He had created us in His image, but the image had been damaged and defaced, and now we were in the fallen image of another.

Just as Boaz said, "There is a kinsman nearer you than me," so Christ could have said to you and me in our situation, "There is a kinsman nearer you than Me. You are *Adam's*, made in his image." Yet in His wonderful grace, this God-made-flesh reaches out His hand to us and offers a relationship that allows for our redemption. When? *As soon as you and I acknowledge that our own human flesh can never redeem us.*

There's the rub. The question mark curves like a serpent: "Will you depend—*fully rely*—on another's power? Will you become a child of grace? The whole story of our society—the twisted, tragic tale of political, military, economic, social, judicial, and environmental chaos—centers in this: We live in a world determined to redeem itself from its problems by the energy of the nearest of kin...the energy of Adam. Rather than turning to the One who came to redeem, the spirit of our world screams, "We will not have this man to reign over us!" (Luke 19:14). But let us learn Ruth's utter dependence—as surely in the details of our life *with* Christ as in our salvation *through* Christ.

✦ ✦ ✦

Notice also, please, that when the man who was nearest of kin to Elimelech realized there was a *widow* in the redemption package, along with the land, he immediately began to backpedal.

"I cannot redeem it," he said. His reason? "Lest I ruin my own inheritance."

In this, we can see a twofold picture of our flesh: It is incapable of redeeming, and it is wrapped up in itself. The kinsman was saying, "Look, if you're just talking about a *field*, then I'll redeem it. But if you're talking about a *relationship*—having to raise a kid who won't even be my own and taking on a wife who might threaten the harmony of our home—then, no, it doesn't sit my order of things. I can't redeem it."

No matter how noble or resourceful any of us may be, we don't have the resources to be a redeemer. And no matter how inclined we may be to care for others, even at our own expense, at some point the flesh crops up and says, "This really isn't convenient for me."

Everything about the flesh wants control—pleads for carnal dominion. The flesh wants to hold on to its own—its own *timing*, its own *authority*, its own *way!*

But flesh cannot redeem flesh. We could never achieve heaven on our own efforts, and neither can we manufacture kingdom life in our own energy. As our Redeemer so kindly and bluntly tells us, "Without Me you can do nothing" (John 15:5). And so it was in that ancient day as well.

Boaz becomes a magnificent Old Testament picture of the One who laid down his self-interest, laid down his reputation, and became a kinsman-redeemer. Ruth is a picture of an outsider who humbled herself before God and found a new home and a new life. Ruth manifests so beautifully that dependence on the Lord that learns to say, "He will take care of it all."

And what came of their union? What came of Ruth's humble dependence on her kinsman-redeemer? A child called "Obed," whose name means "a servant who worships."

Without pressing the point too far, I like to think that's what happens when you open your life up to the Redeemer...when you step back out of the way and allow Him to work in and through your life. He will beget in you a self-forgetting spirit of service and worship. And out of these flow true kingdom power and authority.

Scripture may not tell us what sort of life Obed went on to live, but it does tell us what he *became*...and we need to conclude by looking at the mighty message in his birth. It's an astounding finish to a story that began in such poverty and humility. Which just goes to show...once you allow redemption to begin, you never know where it will end.

$\mathcal{A}$ New Time and A New Place

So Boaz took Ruth and she became his wife; and when he went in to her, the Lord gave her conception, and she bore a son. Then the women said to Naomi, "Blessed be the Lord, who has not left you this day without a near kinsman; and may his name be famous in Israel! And may he be to you a restorer of life and a nourisher of your old age; for your daughter-in-law, who loves you, who is better to you than seven sons, has borne him."

Then Naomi took the child and laid him on her bosom, and became a nurse to him. Also the neighbor women gave him a name, saying, "There is a son born to Naomi." And they called his name Obed. He is the father of Jesse, the father of David. (Ruth 4:13-17)

$\mathcal{A}$ NEW TIME AND A NEW PLACE

Ruth had a baby!

What event could better picture a new time and a new place? What blessing could bring more joy or speak more deeply of the Lord's grace and kindness to a woman of her time?

Daughter, your fullest hour has come. There is nothing but the joy of divine destiny upon you now!

If there had ever been the slightest question in Ruth's mind about her choice to leave Moab behind and cast her lot with the God of Israel, it was answered now! And it was answered in a single word.

Obed.

One word. One child. One announcement of a name. Yet what an opening God made! What a *break-through*—not only for Ruth, but for those who down through the years would dare to hope in God in the face of difficulty and despair.

Obed speaks of *life* where there had been a dead-end street...of *fruitfulness* where there had been famine... of a heaven-sent *breakthrough* where there had been unyielding barriers. And finally, the name Obed speaks of a *future* beyond the eye's ability to measure or the heart's capacity to imagine or dream.

Quite possibly, no other words in the Book of Ruth are more central to its message than the final ten words of the final chapter: "Boaz begot Obed; Obed begot Jesse, and Jesse begot David."

Great drama clings to that terse, abrupt conclusion. The first time a knowledgeable person reads Ruth, he or she comes to the initial statement of this fact (4:17) and must inevitably be caught and *amazed*. The implications of that little slice of genealogy take your breath away.

"Not really!" the heart exclaims with joy. "Do you mean to tell me that Ruth—the alien, the outsider, the hope-emptied soul with nowhere to go but to God— became the great-grandmother of *David*—Israel's greatest king?

How wonderful! No, it's *more* than wonderful. It's so splendidly typical of the loving-kindness and the tender mercies of the Almighty One, our Redeemer. Indeed, the future bursting upon Ruth through the birth of this baby boy is vastly beyond what she ever could have or would have dared to imagine.

Her happiness at the birth might be explained easily enough. What cannot be so easily explained, however, is how a glorious eternal dawn was breaking through this young woman...to touch the rest of history. Cradled in that armful of blessing was a world full of possibilities beyond dreaming.

Obed, who would become the father of Jesse, who would become the father of David, would also become the distant grandparent of yet another renowned son.

The "Son of David." Jesus Christ, Son of the living God.

✦ ✦ ✦

Standing as we are at the dawn of the third millennium since Christ's birth, we're privileged to look back and see the breadth and beauty of this event in Ruth's life. It is like standing at a vista point and looking across the great panorama of the Grand Canyon. And where would we place Ruth in such an analogy? She would be making her way long one of the narrow, winding trails in the depths of the canyon. Excited and joyful as she may have been, she could not see from our vantage point. She could not know what was going to happen.

The eternal God had a plan well beyond her scope or grasp, just as He so often has in our circumstances. Think of it! Baby Obed…that tiny package of fulfillment… would become a pivotal link in Almighty God's coming to earth! Obed's future grandson David would become the king of Israel, and from his seed would rise the One who, in the fullness of time, would be called "Messiah."

Talk about glory! Talk about destiny!

Yet hear me, dear one: God's amazing grace may converge upon our lives just as it descended upon Ruth's. He delights to respond to those who long for a new time and place in their walk with Him. No, the reward may not be immediate. (It took time for the heart of a Moabite girl to orient to Judah.) And no, the harvest may not appear right away. (Gleaning leftovers in the corners of the field preceded the lavish gifts of grain that filled Ruth's shawl to overflowing.)

As a matter of fact, the discoveries of God's redemptive grace in your life may remind you of Ruth's long, cold night on the threshing floor. You may find yourself wondering what will come of your commitment to cling to His promises. And in Ruth's case, even after marrying her kinsman-redeemer, she still had to wait and wonder. Pregnancy takes time!

We too may wonder as we wait. We may say, "How long, O Lord?" And as with those moments before the delivery of a child, we may ask ourselves, "Can I stand the pain until…?"

It seems that so many of God's most fulfilling promises arrive gift wrapped in pain and trial. But equally blessed is the truth that *joy comes in the morning!*

Ruth's baby was delivered, and through him a future beyond comprehension would unfold. Ruth stands as an amazed participant in the sovereign grace that ordains God's purposes—and joys—through human vessels.

It is the way of His Kingdom. It enters *through* people who not only look forward to heaven, but who expect new times and new places of "Kingdom entry" *here*—amid the hard realities of this present world.

◆ ◆ ◆

That's the way it is with the Kingdom of God. We began our study with that emphasis, and again, let's hear the words of Isaiah resound even more deeply in our hearts.

"For My thoughts are not your thoughts,
Nor are your ways My ways . . .
For as the heavens are higher than the earth,
So are My ways higher than your ways,
And My thoughts than your thoughts."
(Isaiah 55:8-9)

To welcome God's entry into the world of our personal experience, each of us will recurrently be called to His *ways*—they are always broader and deeper than we can imagine.

The Father is assuring us—revealing His ways as a promise—that those words *truly abide* in our hearts. This will bring a new readiness to *resist* doubt or fear, or *to* yield to the supposition that God is confined by any circumstance or obstacle. The message of Ruth rises by God's ways that she discovered when she chose a pathway that brought a new time and a new place—via pathways that introduced her to the "Kingdom possibilities" contained in the gracious will, amazing ways, and wonderful works of the King of the Universe—our Almighty Father.

The Outflowing of Kingdom Breakthrough

When David stepped up to the throne of Israel, his kingdom flowed like a mighty river through the land. Yet in all probability, most people overlooked the spring in which that river found its source.

David became known as the king with a "heart after God." But where and how was that heart formed? It didn't happen in a vacuum. David's passion for God and his understanding of the Lord's loving-kindness and gentle mercies must have begun somewhere. But where? We see nothing of that heart in David's father or brothers.

From where did it spring?

Try Great-grandma Ruth!

David, who more than any other character in the Old Testament expressed the love of God, might well have seen that love modeled by his father's father's mother. He would have known the story well! Ruth... the humble immigrant and stranger who left her homeland in hopes of finding better times and a better place. Ruth...who turned her back on old gods and old ways to take shelter under the wings of a God who made and kept His promises.

And so David, the great-grandson of a widowed, destitute foreigner, came into his kingdom.

Kingdom.

The very word breathes of power, sounding upon our lips like the thunder of a Chinese gong. And power is unquestionably involved when the rule of God's Kingdom is mentioned. We exclaim, "Thine is the kingdom *and the power!*"

Obed's birth was an unrecognized revelation of that power. This was a baby born into an era of chaos and violence. Israel was ruled by whim, just as the faithful historian recorded: "Everyone did what was right in his own eyes" (Judges 21:25). Yet even then, in those chaotic, unsettled times, God was setting in motion a series of events that would result in the revelation of

His rule through a king of His pleasure.

It shouldn't surprise us. After all, *it was prophesied at Ruth's wedding!*

> *"May your house be like the house of Perez...because of the offspring which the Lord will give..."* (Ruth 4:12)

Those weren't just nice words to say at a wedding. They were the spoken blessings of the sons and daughters of Abraham, words which they *believed would come true.* And they did, for with what we know of Obed's birth and lineage, we can see that the "Perez Prophecy" was fulfilled.

And it was a prophecy of divine *breakthrough.*

◆ ◆ ◆

The Perez account seems like a "sidebar" in the Book of Genesis. Coming as it does in the midst of the epic story of Joseph, it almost intrudes in the text—as though it really doesn't belong.

Yet Genesis 38 is right where God wants it to be. It is a reminder that although Joseph, the son of Jacob, will rise to unheard-of heights, Messiah will be born into the lineage of Judah, not Joseph. The chapter contains the brief, candid account of a woman unjustly treated by Judah, her father-in-law. It relates his one-night stand with a woman disguised as a harlot—who was actually his own widowed daughter-in-law. Finally, it tells of the birth of twins that resulted from that union.

As the woman was about to deliver, a baby's hand thrust forth from the womb, and the midwife attending immediately tied a strong on the child's wrist. Twins were expected, and no one wanted confusion in the all-important matter of birth order. But surprisingly, the hand pulled back into the womb, and when Twin Number One was finally born, there was no string attached.

"How did you *break through?*" the attendants asked, and the baby was named Perez, or "breakthrough."

In this little story of Perez, positions were reversed, and Number Two somehow became Number One. It *was* a breakthrough—a victory of the underdog—and one ordained by God. In a similar way, the marriage of Ruth to Boaz was a breakthrough—something that just wouldn't have happened in the normal course of events. Wealthy, landed, Israelite men were not in the habit of marrying destitute Moabite widows.

So at the wedding of Boaz and Ruth, the song of the celebrants rang out with real joy—joy for the disenfranchised seeker who had entered into the rich blessing of God. "May the offspring from this bride be like Perez!"

It's a song that vibrates from the depth of the human spirit; it's the chant that rises from a stadium in the interest of the underdog. It is the song of the Gospel and the message of the Kingdom of God: "Let the hopeless find hope; let the broken be healed; let the oppressed go free!"

◆ ◆ ◆

What is it about the Kingdom of God that offers such a promise of "breakthrough"?

It is not a matter of fortune or luck; it is a matter of love. Eternal love which shines from a cross and an empty tomb. Once Jesus died in our place and rose again to God's right hand, *there is no power of defeat or distress that cannot be reversed!* Listen…if death itself can be swallowed up in life, then every dead-end street in our sin-darkened world can be broken through! God's pathway of promise becomes a living highway of Kingdom victory.

The Kingdom comes with the King—and all of us who have welcomed Him into our hearts have reason to rejoice, however trying our situation. Ruth—a widow who had no money, no home, no country of her own, and yet found a land, a living God, and a loving husband—gave birth to a son and an heir.

It is the way of the King. He reverses situations. He turns impossibilities on their heads. He transforms darkness into dazzling light and snatches life from the very claws of the grave.

His name is Jesus, Jesus; sad hearts weep no more.
He has healed the brokenhearted, opened wide the prison door.
He is able to deliver evermore!

✦ ✦ ✦

Ruth's new time and place brought about a union. And from that union came a child. And from that tiny child's yet-undeveloped loins would come the seed that would bring physical life to Israel's greatest king…and later to the Savior of the whole world.

The point is this; If we have received His life-gift of love and forgiveness, within that new birthing we received the seed of His Kingdom's breakthrough power as well.

Yes…the power to snap the confining ropes of our past and redeem us to eternal life. *But more than that.*

Yes…the power to break the grip of death and bring us to heaven's eternal joys. *But more than that.*

The timeless and unlimited hope of every believer is woven through a little book of the Bible called "Ruth." And as we relive the story of a Moabite girl who fled death and famine to seek life and fruitfulness and the eternal God, we sense an invitation in our own hearts. It is an invitation from the same Holy Spirit who inspired the Book of Ruth—and made sure it was recorded.

What was it Paul said in the Book of Romans?

Such things were written in the Scriptures long ago to teach us. They give us hope and encouragement as we wait patiently for God's promises. (15:4 NLT)

He recorded it for you and me! He recorded it so that the truth of her story might sustain us in whatever hardship or heartache we face through the passing years. He recorded it so we might experience the mighty breakthrough power of His Kingdom in our lives, just as Ruth experienced it so many years ago.

He wants Ruth's transcendent victory to become our own "amazing grace" triumph in life!

I can't let go of my pen without reaching with my other hand to take yours—to draw you as close to this truth as you'll come...right now. Our study of Ruth's adventure was never intended to be merely inspirational. No, it's meant to be *incarnational*—taking on flesh-and-blood reality in your own situation, right now. He intends His Word in Ruth's story to become His Spirit's power in yours.

So let's conclude this book together as a people who reach with open hands to heaven in *praise* for God's great love...and then with open hearts in *readiness* to receive His promise.

His new time is now.

His new place is here.

Here and now—where each of us is at this very moment. Whatever the struggle, whatever the stress, and whatever our sense of "worthiness" might be. If Ruth teaches us anything, it is God's delight to meet the one who simply *comes*...seeking.

Come with me now...in prayer.

Dear Father, I am warmed within by Your Holy Spirit of promise, whose presence has drawn me into Your Word of Truth. In Jesus' name, I come to thank You.

Thank You for the truth that NOTHING can frustrate Your purpose toward me. NOTHING can blockade the possibilities of Your loving intent for my life being fulfilled. As I have read of Ruth, one of Your daughters of long ago, You have convinced me of Your care for me, one of Your children, in the here and now. I put my case before You, not on the grounds of my worthiness, but on the foundation of the cross which has purchased my salvation and all that I need pertaining to my life as one of Your own...

Now, dear one, speak your heart. Indeed, let me urge you to write in the following space the essence of your own heart's cry for a new time, a new place, *or both and more!*

A NEW TIME AND A NEW PLACE

MY HEART'S CRY FOR A NEW TIME AND A NEW PLACE

_____

_____

_____

_____

_____

_____

_____

_____

_____

_____

_____

_____

_____

_____

_____

_____

_____

_____

_____

_____

_____

_____

_____

Now...let's conclude our prayer together.

So, dear Father, I commit these words of my heart's hope to you. And just as Ruth's path involved time and trial before her fullest hopes were tangibly fulfilled, I will simply rest my case with You and wait for You to act on my behalf.

You are the Father of my hope and my salvation, and Your Son is the Author and Finisher of my faith. As Your own child, and with Jesus as my Lord, I now move forward to live in the realm of Your Kingdom's new possibilities for me...

> *at this new time of trust,*
> *and in this new place of rest.*
>
> *Amen*